Eastern Magic
and
Western Spiritualism

By Henry S. Olcott

Copyright © 2021 Lamp of Trismegistus. All rights reserved. No part of this publication may be reproduced or transmitted in any form or by any means, electronic or mechanical, including photocopying, recording, or by any information storage and retrieval system, without permission in writing from Lamp of Trismegistus. Reviewers may quote brief passages.

ISBN: 978-1-63118-584-7

Esoteric Classics

Other Books in this Series and Related Titles

Aurora of the Philosophers by Paracelsus (978-1-63118-507-6)

Clairvoyance and Psychic Abilities by A Besant &c (978-1-63118-403-1)

The Feminine Occult by various authors (978-1-63118-711-7)

Rosicrucian Rules, Secret Signs, Codes and Symbols by various (978-1-63118-488-8)

An Outline of Theosophy by C W Leadbeater (978-1-63118-452-9)

Paracelsus, the Four Elements and Their Spirits by M P Hall (978-1-63118-400-0)

Essays on Ancient Magic by Helena P Blavatsky (978-1-63118-535-9)

Essays on the Esoteric Tradition of Karma by A Besant &c (978-1-63118-426-0)

The Use of Evil by Annie Besant (978-1-63118-532-8)

Occult Arts by William Q. Judge (978-1-63118-559-5)

The Alchemical Catechism of Paracelsus by Paracelsus (978-1-63118-513-7)

Alchemy in the Nineteenth Century by Helena P Blavatsky (978-1-63118-446-8)

Qabbalistic Teachings and the Tree of Life by M P Hall (978-1-63118-482-6)

The Historic, Mythic and Mystic Christ by Annie Besant (978–1–63118–533–5)

The Hidden Mysteries of Christianity by Annie Besant (978–1–63118–534–2)

History, Analysis and Secret Tradition of the Tarot by Hall &c (978-1-63118-445-1)

Kali the Mother by Sister Nivedita (978-1-63118-558-8)

Arcane Formulas or Mental Alchemy by W W Atkinson (978-1-63118-459-8)

The Machinery of the Mind by Dion Fortune (978-1-63118-451-2)

Vision of the Spirit by C. Jinarajadasa (978-1-63118-560-1)

The Leadbeater Reader: A Selection of Occult Essays (978-1-63118-483-3)

Audio versions are also available on Audible, Amazon and Apple

Other Books in this Series and Related Titles

Spiritual Progress and Practical Occultism by H P Blavatsky (978–1–63118–583–0)

Memory and Consciousness by Besant & Blavatsky (978–1–63118–582–3)

The Origin of Evil by Helena P Blavatsky (978–1–63118–581–6)

The Camp of Philosophy: Studies in Alchemy by Bloomfield (978–1–63118–580–9)

The Testaments of the Twelve Patriarchs (978–1–63118–579–3)

Occult or Exact Science? by Helena P Blavatsky (978–1–63118–578–6)

Occultism, Semi-Occultism & Pseudo Occultism by A Besant (978–1–63118–577–9)

The Fourth-Gospel and Synoptical Problem by G R S Mead (978–1–63118–576–2)

On the Bhagavad-Gita by T Subba Row &c (978–1–63118–575–5)

What Theosophy Does for Us by C W Leadbeater (978–1–63118–574–8)

Spiritual Life for Man by Annie Besant (978–1–63118–573–1)

The Mysteries by Annie Besant (978–1–63118–572–4)

Fundamental Ideas of Theosophy by Bhagwan Das (978–1–63118–571–7)

Dreams: What They Are and Caused by C W Leadbeater (978–1–63118–570–0)

Communication Between Different Worlds by Annie Besant (978–1–63118–569–4)

Animism, Magic and the Omnipotence of Thought by S Freud (978–1–63118–568–7)

Buddhism by F Otto Schrader (978–1–63118–567–0)

Death by W W Westcott (978–1–63118–566–3)

The Religion of Theosophy by Bhagwan Das (978–1–63118–565–6)

The Spirit of Zoroastrianism by Henry S Olcott (978–1–63118–564–9)

The Brotherhood of Religions by Annie Besant (978–1–63118–563–2)

Audio versions are also available on Audible, Amazon and Apple

Table of Contents

Introduction…7

Eastern Magic & Western Spiritualism…9

Occultism is not the acquirement of powers, whether psychic or intellectual, though both are its servants. Neither is occultism the pursuit of happiness, as men understand the word; for the first step is sacrifice, the second, renunciation. Occultism is the science of life, the art of living.

INTRODUCTION

The word "esoteric" can be difficult to define. Esotericism in general can be seen less as a system of beliefs and more as a category, which encompasses numerous, different systems of beliefs. It's a bit of juxtaposition, since the word "esoteric" indicates something that few people know about, while the term itself broadly covers numerous philosophies, practices, areas of study and belief systems.

In a greater sense, Esotericism acts as a storehouse for secret knowledge, which is often considered ancient (by *tradition, if not by fact),* passed down from generation to generation, in private. At various times in history, simply possessing the knowledge of some of these subjects, was considered illegal and a jailable offence, if discovered. This usually included such general topics as Alchemy, Pharmacology, Qabalah, Hermeticism, Occultism, Ceremonial Magic, Astrology, Divination, Rosicrucianism and so on. Collectively, these areas of study were often referred to as the esoteric sciences.

Sometimes, the outer garment of a subject isn't esoteric, while what is hidden beneath it, is. As an example, Freemasonry isn't necessarily esoteric by nature (at *least not anymore),* but certain signs, passwords and handshakes given to the candidate during their initiation, are in fact, esoteric, in the sense that they are hidden from the general public.

Today, in the twenty-first century, such topics are readily available at bookstores across the country, and numerous mainsteam publishers offer beginners guides and coffee-table volumes on many of these subjects, intended for mass appeal. Books like *"The Secret"* have turned previously arcane topics into household knowledge. All that being the case, however, it isn't to say that there still aren't buried secrets to uncover, ancient wisdom being ignored and forgotten mysteries to be explored. In fact, it is often that we are only able to further our own studies by standing on the shoulders of these disappearing giants.

Lamp of Trismegistus is doing its part to help preserve humanity's esoteric history by making some of these classics available to those students who are seeking to unearth the knowledge of these ancient colossi.

So, be sure to check other titles from our *Esoteric Classics* series, as well as our *Occult Fiction, Theosophical Classics, Foundations of Freemasonry Series, Supernatural Fiction, Paranormal Research Series, Studies in Buddhism* and our *Christian Apocrypha Series.* You can also download the audio versions of most of these titles from Amazon, Apple or Audible, for learning on the go.

EASTERN MAGIC AND WESTERN SPIRITUALISM

by Henry S. Olcott

Absurd as it would appear to an ancient Theurgist who might be permitted to re-visit the earth, it requires a certain degree of moral courage to avow oneself, in this Nineteenth Century, a believer in the possibility of magical phenomena. To assert that there was a broad foundation of fact for old-time myths; that the hidden world can be made visible by the scientific processes of Magic; that it is as thickly peopled as the outer one; that its races are subject to the empire of law; that over many of them, man has a natural dominion; that each fills a place, and furnishes a link in the cosmic chain of Evolution, quite as real and as necessary as Man himself - is to render oneself liable to the contempt of Modern Science, the anathemas of the clergy, and the derision of contemporary fools.

Well, be it so. I risk the contempt, the anathemas and the derision; and shall do my best to deserve each and all, by plainness of speech and a statement of the truth. Since it is inevitable that public men who avow a belief in any unfashionable philosophy or creed shall be slandered and otherwise assailed, it will not be my fault if I do not give the enemies of Occultism and Spiritualism, something to ponder over and explain away. There is a sweet satisfaction in knowing that, after admitting all that can be said about the Mysticism of the one and the frauds of the other, both can bettor afford to enter into the field of controversy than either of their antagonists. The Occultist can point to the irrefragable proof that every existing religion is the direct descendant of ancient theogonies, and the Spiritualist cite from historical records, the evidence that his phenomena are as old as the race itself. Let the clergy swagger as they will and enjoy their brief hour of authority; and let fanciful philosophical systems be hatched from the inner consciousness of our *Esprits-forts* - they only come and go like the moths of summer; while the Past broods over us with the monuments of its wisdom and the glory of its inspiration, making us feel the nothingness of modern scientific and religious thought!

We cannot take in this idea of the relative superiority of antiquity to ourselves until we disabuse our minds of a very great and a very common fallacy. We have been accustomed to compare our own freedom and enlightenment with the intellectual night of the Middle Ages, and to deduce therefrom the idea that the progression of the race is invariably from lower to higher planes in an oblique line upward. From the stone age to our own Epoch, we have been taught to believe, the evolution has been constant and upward. There have been no breaks, no retrocessions, no backward swings of the pendulum. The noonday brightness of our day and the dim twilight of the remote past, shut in at last by a midnight blackness of ignorance and barbarism, has been the favourite figure of many an orator, the theme of many a poet. What was lacking to corroborate this theory, so grateful to the pride of our century, seemed to be supplied in the relics of the flint age, the caves of Kent, the Locustrines, the Mound-builders, the Druids, the prehistoric house-building races of North and South America and the rude remains of the Ptolemaic Egyptians. If any occasional discovery in archaeology or geology seemed to indicate a flaw in the theory, and to attack the foundation of somebody's claim to honor as an original discoverer, or the orthodoxy of somebody's creed as a direct revelation to some modern mystic, it was by common consent put aside as intrusive, if not false; and the discoverer called Atheist or Quack as the case might be.

But, by a beneficent law of the Universe - which itself is the most complete embodiment of Divine law - Truth is so mighty, that, in the long run, it prevails. It is the iron pot floating down stream amid the pots of clay, breaking them one by one, in spite of their buoyancy, and the beauty of their exterior decoration. The archeologists and geologists responded to the taunts of their critics by working twice as hard and digging twice as deep; and so it has finally happened that we are getting from underground, proof which none can gainsay; that geology is a more infallible revelation of the Creator's Will than the Bible, and that human progress, instead of being in a direct line, has been in circles.

The exhumations and surface remains in Egypt and Asia show us that long before the time of the Pharaohs and Ptolemies, the Arts and Sciences had reached a perfection to which even we are strangers; and that they gradually decayed and were lost to the historical Epochs which superficial writers erroneously call Antiquity. Below the strata of the Abbott and Lepsius discoveries, Marriette Bey has found specimens of art which, according to Taylor, compare with the most renowned productions of the Athenian school; and it was but the other day that Ebers translated from a papyrus, recipes for the very lotions, dyes and pigments employed by the American girl of the period, to-disfigure herself in the eyes of every true artist and connoisseur.

We pride ourselves upon the Capitol at Washington, the Louvre, the Houses of Parliament, the Duomo of Milan, St. Peter's at Rome, the Thames Tunnel, the Suez Canal; and point to them with pride as triumphs of architectural skill; but, in comparison with the ruins of Karnak and Luxor with the Pyramids and the Sphinx, with the Labyrinth and lake Meuris, they appear like insignificant child-work. Says Champollion (whose life was passed in Egypt, and whose accuracy of statement is unchallenged): " No people of ancient or modern time has conceived of the art of architecture upon a scale so sublime - so grandiose - as it existed among the Ancient Egyptians; and the imagination, which in Europe soars far above our porticos, arrests itself and falls helpless at the feet of the 140 columns of the Hypostyle of Karnak." In one of the halls of the Temple, and that not the longest, the cathedral of Notre Dame would occupy only a corner; while the area of its walls was so vast as to include artificial mountains and lakes of great size. Herodotus, who lived five centuries before Christ; who is styled the "Father of History," and of whom the *Encyclopedia Britannica* says: "No traveler ever possessed in a higher degree than he, the power of sifting what he observed, of preserving what was valuable, and rejecting what was silly and useless, was permitted to examine some of the chambers of the Labyrinth which were above ground; but the 1,500 subterranean ones, being the sepulchers of the Kings, were kept sacred from the visits of the profane. The walls and ceilings of all these apartments were painted in colors which even in our day retain their pristine beauty, and adorned with sculptures so exquisitely minute that it needs a magnifying glass to trace their details. View these remains, recall the teeming multitudes which peopled the Nile Delta, see their Engineers, their Architects, their Astronomers, their Artificers, their Sculptors, at work; compare them with the tattered shepherds and nomadic Bedouin robbers who now roam that solitary district, and you may have some conception of the truth that we move in cycles.

Again, turn to Prescott's histories of Mexico and Peru, to Stephens's explorations in Central America, and to Catherwood's drawings of the remains of the Quiché nations, and the strongest corroborative proof will again be found of the existence of the same law. What are the degenerate Mexicans, Peruvians, and Yucatanese of the present day in comparison with the ancient peoples who erected the mighty temples of Palanque and Uxmal and plated the roof of those at Cuzco and Arequipa with gold?

But I am not pronouncing a discourse upon Archaeology, and so I will leave this highly suggestive portion of the subject. It must be observed, however, that as there is nothing in human experience to indicate that the intellect of man tends to abnormal and monstrous growths, but everything on the contrary to show that its powers are always maintained in equilibrium - the spiritual keeping pace, on the average, with the rational - it would be the height of absurdity to suppose that people who could arrive at such supreme development in the arts and physical sciences should not have proportionately perfected their religious systems. As we have seen psychology keeping abreast of physics in the observation of natural law; and a belief in miracle growing weaker in proportion to the foundation of libraries and museums and the establishment of laboratories and observatories, so it must have been in the days of old.

It does violence to every analogy deducible from observations of our fellow-men, to say, that intellects capable of projecting and executing such works as those whose ruins may still be seen, would consent to limit their inquiry to the laws of physical nature, and leave those of the spiritual world unstudied. Would philosophers, competent according to Draper, to calculate an eclipse within a few seconds of the truth; to catalogue the stars and know their emplacement and occultations; to fix the length of the sidereal and tropical years; to discover the precession of the equinoxes; would any intellectual growth capable of giving to humanity an Aristotle, a Pythagoras, an Archimedes, a Ptolemy Soter, leave any corner of Nature un-searched? And do you suppose that such intellects as these, whose superior has not since been seen, were not as capable of unraveling the secrets of the Universe as our Tyndalls and Huxleys, our Comtes and Herbert Spencers ?

Let us see what these old philosophers did know of the spiritual half of the Cosmos.

He who would analyze the ancient creeds and arrive at their true significance must constantly bear in mind that words and symbols were employed in ancient times as veils to cover ideas. Under the form of parables and romances, there lay truths of great importance; just as the records of Egypt are concealed from the superficial observer behind the hieroglyphs of their temples, and the hieratic (or priestly) writings of their papyri. Knowledge was almost wholly confined to the privileged class of priests, who were at once scientific experimentalists and religious teachers. They were again subdivided into classes and sections, to each of which was confided some particular study; and all were in subordination to a supreme head, as the Catholic Clergy is subject to the Bishop of Rome. Observe that as both scientific and religious investigations were under their direction, it was but a natural precaution that they should clothe their wisdom in such an artful outer garb, as should prevent its becoming known to the vulgar multitude, who were unfitted to make a. proper use of it. Observe, further, that it was inevitable that when the adepts of this esoteric wisdom should be dispersed, the mask alone would remain; and the secret to the hidden knowledge could only be found after an amount of labor and research at least equal to that which was originally required to conceal it. This accounts for all the misunderstanding which has prevailed respecting the scientific and religious knowledge of the Ancients; as well as for the cheap contempt felt for those who in various subsequent epochs have tried to do justice to their memory.

It is as gross a piece of ignorance to confound the animal and vegetable worship of the Egyptians with its real significance, or the mythological gods of Greece and Rome with their real meaning, as to fancy that no one discovered this continent before Columbus, or the properties of the Universal Ether before the authors of The Unseen Universe. The Hindu Pantheon is peopled with millions of spiritual entities and individual gods; but Hindu, Egyptian and Greek, like their predecessor, the Chaldean, had for the basis of their Esoteric philosophy, the idea of one Supreme, Creative Power, endowed with countless attributes. It was these attributes which in their Oriental habit of parable, they typified as separate deities. The Gods of the Grecian Olympus were but symbolical representations of the forces of Nature; and in their turn, these forces in their ultimate analysis were but the varying manifestations of one primal force; having dual properties and a perfect equilibrium.

The most ancient philosophy known to us is the Chaldean, and this taught the idea that when the Supreme Intelligence desired to manifest itself outwardly - it sent out from itself an emanation - a creative principle - which, by virtue of its inherent impulse, evolved everything out of Chaos. This principle was called by various names; and Chaos itself, which our modern scientists know as the UNIVERSAL ETHER, they called PHTHA. The Egyptians knew it under the name of RA; the Hindus as BRAHM; the Zoroastrian Persians, as ORMUZD; the Assyrians, as ATHOR; and the Greeks as JUPITER. But, however called, it was one and the same thing, after all; and identically the same as the Universal Ether, from which the most conservative of our astronomers now tell us the whole planetary system has been evolved.

The ancients knew it as a principle having two parts - light and shadow, matter and spirit - each of which was the complement of the other, and both in exact balance. In a wonderfully erudite work which the Russian lady, Madame Blavatsky, is now writing, occurs a curious quotation from the Chaldean *Book of Numbers*, which shows beyond question that not only was the sphericity of the planets known in the prehistoric period, but also the law of the birth and death of worlds, so charmingly told by my friend and correspondent, Mr. Proctor, in his various works.

All the nations above referred to, gave names not only to each of the two sides of Nature, but also to the separate manifestations of the forces inherent in them; and in due course of time, when, owing to political disorders and the devastations of war, the hieratic schools of the true adepts were broken up, these names became identified with personalities, and people worshipped them as gods and goddesses. Thus were the several mythologies developed, one by one, and the philosophical conception of the one Supreme Power lost from view.

It was taught in all these theogonies that the spiritual side of Nature passes through a process of evolution which exactly keeps pace with the evolution in the material side - no orb of gross matter being formed without an interior, vivifying orb of Spirit; no plant or animal produced without an inner plant or animal so to speak, within the casing; and no man without a spiritual body within the substance of his physical body. As the progress of planetary growth is, first, an aggregation of star-dust, or cosmic molecules, into a nucleus, then, a fiery cloudlet, then a vast haze, then a spiral and spheroidal formation, then, the ultimate condensation of a solid globe, from whose particles every form of life is gradually evolved; so the ancients believed that the perfected human spirit was only the apex of a pyramid, whose base covered all space, and whose successive layers were composed of an infinite variety of organized spiritual entities. They were far more consistent evolutionists than we, for in their scheme there was no " missing link ".

It was a fundamental doctrine with them that, as immortal man is the apex of this pyramid, he controls what lies beneath him, by right of his superior spiritual perfection, he having what the antecedent beings have not, an immortal soul. This immortal soul they believed to be a spark of the Divine, Creative Soul; and, as the whole is but an aggregation of parts, and parts resemble the whole, Man, in their judgment, was the lord of the lesser Universe, the Microcosm. To exercise this imperial rule, he needed three things: To KNOW; to DARE; to WILL: and as this knowledge might be perverted to the most fearful results if wielded with an evil purpose, or ignorantly, a fourth condition was imposed: to KEEP SILENT.

The most superficial observer of natural phenomena must have thought of the havoc which might be wrought by any one who could bring on tempests, whirlwinds, lightning-strokes or pestilence, at will. When such persons feel like complaining of the secretiveness and parables of the adepts in Magic, let them pause, and reflect on what would happen if the criminal classes knew how to control, at their pleasure, Magnetism and Electricity, and the other natural forces amenable to the control of the will- power. And, if the secrets of the ancient magicians were published, what would prevent their employment by such people for the destruction of society ? You have all seen mesmeric experiments, wherein one strong will exercises absolute power over many weaker ones; where the subject loses control over his sensations, bodily functions, his memory, and his imagination. While under the spell, he can absolutely be made to do anything tho operator chooses; and I have heard of cases where convulsions and death have been caused by over-positiveness, on one side, or over-sensitiveness, on the other. Now fancy for one moment what would happen if every one who chose could learn the secret by which the Eastern Magicians can kill animals by looking at them, and slay men, by intently concentrating their devilish will upon them, although far distant.

A Catholic author, the Chevalier de Mousseaux, tells of a French peasant, named Jacques Pellissier, who gained a livelihood by killing little birds at twenty paces distance, by his will-power; and

17

before the eye of an Indian Adept, the most ferocious beast will fly in terror. Suppose a bad man to possess this power - whose life or fortune would be safe ?

Neither Eastern Magic nor Western Spiritualism can be understood, until one has carefully studied the phenomena of Animal Magnetism, or Mesmerism. To know the rationale of either, one must understand the fact that from one brain to another a subtle fluid can be sent; that, when this connection is once made, unspoken thoughts are transmitted as freely as they are along the wires of a telegraph; and then he must learn what this subtle fluid is, and how it can best be collected, and directed to accomplish the desired result.

Now the Ancients knew all this; and the Eastern nations of our own day - who are simply practicing what they have learnt from the Ancients - are as familiar with these occult forces as they are with their a, b, c. In fact, they are more so, for the fakirs, of whose magical powers such marvelous stories are told, are often perfectly illiterate. What they know of magic they have inherited from their fathers before them, who, in their turn, had it from their own fathers.

Magic, which simply means *Wisdom*, has two sides - black and white, corresponding to the two sides of nature. WHITE MAGIC deals with white, or light, or *good*, spirits; and Black with the dark, or *bad* ones. Remember what I said of the opposing powers of Nature, and you will see how perfectly reasonable it is that, in the progress of Evolution, races of opposing, or, as we say, *evil* spirits, should be produced as well as races of good ones. How, otherwise, could the balance of the world be maintained ?

The Hierophants of the ancient temples, and the worthy priests of Nature who, under many names - Theurgists, Theosophists, Neo-Platonists, Gnostics, Essenians, Hermetists, Rosicrucians - have passed the divine secrets down the ages, practiced White Magic: the whole infernal line of Sorcerers, Necromancers, and Obi-men, Black Magic.

White Magic is a moral touchstone, which tests the purity, unselfishness, faith and courage of its adepts as the *aqua-regia* does the purity of gold. No debauchee, no miser, no coward, no glutton cam be a Magician. Such as these take refuge in Sorcery; whose arts enable them to conjure about them the debased and unprogressed spirits of men, and the soulless beings of the Elements. For a while they may riot in pleasure and enjoy wealth unbounded; but the day inevitably comes when their once potent wills grow enfeebled by indulgence, and they fall a prey to the infernal intelligences once so pliant and complaisant. The wretched victim dies by his own hand, or by some appalling catastrophe, and " the latter end of that man is worse than the first."

To give an idea of what is meant by Magical practice, I will say, that those who have been initiated can concentrate and project against a given point, the subtle forces of Nature, and command the assistance of the beings which dwell in the universal Ether, or Astral Light. These beings are divided by the Kabalists into four principal classes—Sylphs, Gnomes, Undines and Salamanders; each of which has been evolved out of a particular element, and therefore are grouped under the general head of Elementary Spirits.

Some weeks ago I gave a hint of the existence of such beings, and warned my fellow-investigators of Spiritualistic phenomena not to be deceived into mistaking them for real human beings, even when they should appear like them in materialized form. Dear me I how much sport it made. People who apparently had never read a page of Ennemoser or Howitt, of Levi, Salverte or Des Mousseaux - all modern authors - to say nothing of the Hermetist writers of the Middle Ages, the classics of Greece and Rome, or the Hindu or

Egyptian books, fell upon me, tooth and nail, and denounced me as a renegade to the true faith! I was even charged with conspiracy to cheat the public; and one genius, who lives not fifty miles from New York, made himself ridiculous in the eyes of both gods and men by hinting that I was a Secret Emissary of the Church of Rome! That capped the climax; and after hearing this, I concluded that it was high time that I should set to work in earnest to let what little light I could upon a subject dark enough to breed such croaking birds of night.

By one of those coincidences which some people call Special Providence, it happened that I had not long to wait before seeing the public possessed of corroborative proof in the related experience of one who, both as a lady and Spiritualist is highly respected in two hemispheres - Mrs. Emma Hardinge Britten. In the Banner of Light, she published accounts of having seen these very elementaries in the mines of England and Bohemia; and, within the past few days, a letter has been received from that noble man and nobleman, Councilor Aksakoff, the Russian Spiritualist, in which he states that Prince Dolgorouky, the great mesmerist, has become fully satisfied that they play a great part in the phenomena of our circles.

Elam, in his *Physician's Problems*, says that the seeds of vice and crime lie just beneath the surface of society, ready to spring up in a moment; and so, when I see how within the past few months the press of Europe and America has fallen to discussing Eastern Magic, in its various aspects, I feel as if, like another Cadmus, I had sown a handful of dragon-teeth, and they had sprung up a host of armed men, to back me and carry me through an opposition that every day grows weaker and weaker.

What is it that the illiberal among Spiritualists object to in Eastern Magic ? Its physical phenomena ? But do not these corroborate their own claim that such physical effects can be produced, and only produced, by an application of the Occult forces of Nature? Its demonstration that these phenomena are within human control, and that more beautiful and surprising effects can be produced than we have seen, or get in any of our 1 circles' ? But does not this immensely add to the dignity of the mind of man, and show us what majestic possibilities lie within its grasp ?

Is it at the idea that there are such beings as Elementary Spirits ? But does not this fact complete the broken chain of Darwin, and show us that one sublime law extends throughout Nature, from the beginning until now ? Do they complain that it shocks the imagination to think that the forms of our beloved dead can be simulated by creatures not much higher than monkeys, in intelligence, nor more morally responsible ? Surely this ought, on the contrary, to make them see the necessity to learn all they can of these races, how to guard against their wiles, circumscribe their power for mischief, and compel them to be our servants, instead of our masters!

If it is more agreeable to any to go on another thirty years as blindly as we have these past thirty, giving our mediums to be the sport and slaves of beings whose approach we cannot prevent, whose presence we cannot recognize until it is too late, and whose infernal swindles and lies we cannot detect until the cause has received grievous injury - if there be any such, let them do as they like. My course is clear: I moan to follow up this subject until I master it, no matter how long it takes nor what labor it involves, I want LIGHT, and I know it can be had.

It is confessed by all thoughtful men that Modern Spiritualism is attended by many mysteries. There are many things that cannot be explained satisfactorily by any philosophy commonly known. I might go further yet, and say that, by the common consent of our philosophers, the same rule holds with most of the physical sciences. But let us confine ourselves to Spiritualism.

It is the universal opinion that the law of attraction holds good throughout everything - like attracts like. This must be true. It st true. Now, will any tell me why a pure girl-medium, tenderly nurtured, modest and self respectful, should at times become horribly profane and indecent when under influence ? If like attracts like, what should attract so vile a spirit to the pure atmosphere of this virgin sibyl ? Why should she not attract strong and good spirits, and repel the evil ones; as her nature, in the normal state, would repel a drunkard and debauchee ? Again: Why should a truthful and honest man, upon becoming a medium, give lying communications, for weeks together; and why should virtuous men and women fall into licentious ways, and yield themselves up to the lusts of the flesh ? Is there no protecting Power to shield the good from the dominion of the bad ? Is the Universe so ill-governed that people can be forcibly made everything that is vile, by other *people* who can approach and poison them unawares ? What becomes of the belief in guardian-angels, common to most who accept the doctrine of an intercourse between this world and the inner one ?

And, to push an enquiry still further: Can the spirits of all human beings assume the appearances of all other human beings at will, so that a returning trickster can pass from circle to circle— personating Washington here, Franklin there, and twenty different celebrities in twenty other places? It it likely that any of these great men would subject themselves to the insults of drunken committee men, the abuse of stolidly ignorant" skeptics," and the repulsive personalities of some mediums, to give tests and exhibit phenomena, every evening of the year, fill over the world, to thousands of inquisitive persons, who go to circles as they would to the circus, to see the fun, (and " dead-head " if they can) ? Now I leave it to candid men to ponder upon this matter. Put yourselves in the place of the educated materialistic investigator, and see how *he* would proceed to argue the case in court: look at the flaws, and see how they can be mended.

Admit that the Elementaries can come floating in upon us in the currents of the Astral Light; that they can handle Magnetism and Electricity as we do water and clay; that they can saturate a medium with it if he is passive and ignorant of their presence, until he becomes, so to speak, dead drunk with it, and as helpless to defend himself as the sot in the gutter; that, being composed of the elements, they can employ them - as we employ fire and water, earth and air, for various purposes by the help of mechanical contrivances; that they can read our thoughts as we read a book, and so frame answers to suit themselves; that, having no consciences, they incline as naturally and easily to what we call wrong, as to right, and make their poor victims, the mediums, the same; - realize these facts, and the mystery is cleared up. I call these *facts because* they are so. They have been proved, hundreds and hundreds of times, by the adepts of magic; and there is not a traveler who need return from India or Egypt without having seen them verified, by ocular demonstration.

Several numbers of the London *Spiritualist* have contained accounts of some of the phenomena witnessed in India by Scientists of European reputation. Of these I select one which shows us a fakir at work. It is by Dr. Maximilian Perty, Professor of Physical Science, and narrates the experiments of a French Scientist named Jacolliot.

"The fakir performs his feats in daylight, in the courtyard of the bungalow. He calls for seven glasses and some garden mould; fills the glasses with it; sticks in each a piece of bamboo, over which he drops some fig-leaves, each perforated with a hole in the centre large enough to admit the stick. The fakir, standing four paces distant, points his hand towards the leaves, remains motionless for sometime, and lo ! the leaves flutter and rise up the sticks, to their tops, and fall back motionless. The atmosphere is perfectly still; it cannot be an effect of the wind; Jacolliot passes between the fakir and the pots - it is not done by fine threads. The phenomenon is repeated, over and over again, the fakir showing entire readiness to vary the experiments in any desired way. Seven clean glasses are then brought and fresh mould, and Jacolliot himself prepares them. The same result happens. He then has holes bored in a new plank, inserts the sticks, places the leaves over them. The same result again, and so it continued for two hours. The fakir then offered to give him a communication from any deceased friend he might think of. Jacolliot throws into a bag a lot of copper types that he had with him, and, picking them out one after another, without looking at them, the leaves rise and fall as certain letters come out, and the result is found to be the following sentence: "*Albain Brunier, mort à Bourg-en-Bresse, 3 Janvier, 1856*"—which was the name and time and place of decease of the friend of whom he thought. That day, and upon fourteen successive ones, Jacolliot tested this spirit in every way he could devise; and he found that, while the arbitrary ms-spellings of the name which he fixed in his mind would be indicated by the movements of the leaves, as if to humor his fancy, they obstinately continued to spell the place of decease correctly, despite his every effort to mislead the invisible intelligence. Clearly, the case proved that the phenomenon was *not* the effect of his own will or imagination; and equally clear it was that the fakir demonstrated his control over a physical, occult force sufficient to move the fig-leaves at a distance of several paces. At the last sitting, "the fakir made the empty plate of a scale sink under a peacock's feather, while the other was weighted with 80 kilos (about 200 lbs.); by a simple placing of his hands on a wreath of flowers it rose in the air, indistinct voices were heard, and an ethereal hand wrote luminous signs in the air". Says Professor Perty: " In the above material phenomena no deception could be discovered, in spite of the severest testing." M. Jacolliot, as the result of his Indian experiments, now " believes that in nature and in man, who is but an atom in the world, there exist boundless forces whose laws are as yet unknown, but which will be discovered; that in the future things will be proved to be realities that are now held to be delusions, and that phenomena will appear which we cannot now so much as imagine."

If there are any present who have read my work entitled *People from the Other World*, they may recall some experiments made by me at Chittenden and at Havana, N.Y., to test this power of the intelligence controlling the occult forces to make a scale-beam sensibly vary with each of a series of weighings of the same spirit, within a few minutes. At Chittenden, Honto's weight varied from 88 to 58, to 88 again, and then to 65 lbs; and at Havana, where I had test conditions, the materialized girl-spirit varied from 77 to 59, and then to 52 lbs. In neither case was there more than 10 minutes from the beginning to the end of the experiment. My idea was to test the theory that a spirit could increase or diminish at will the weight of the matter which it condensed to form its own body. I also experimented with the muscular contraction which could be exerted by a detached spirit-hand upon a spring-balance, both in a vertical and a horizontal direction - I holding the medium's own hands to prevent fraud. In one case, the hand pulled 40 lbs. horizontally; and in the other 50 lbs. vertically. This fact should be noted, for it goes to show that the pulling was not done by the medium, as was insinuated by certain persons, since, in such case, the horizontal pull would of necessity have been stronger than the other, owing to the position the medium occupied.

The other evening Mrs. Youngs, the piano-lifting medium, was tested before the Theosophical Society, and one of the Committee, who lifted the end of the instrument twice in succession - once while the medium stood back from it and ordered the spirits to make it heavier - declared to us that there was a very great difference in the weight.

Take the Indian experiment of the feather, and these of mine together, and they clearly demonstrate that persons in and out of the body can concentrate and direct an invisible force, so as to make objects weigh light or heavy as they choose.

And, again, as to Jacolliot's wreath-experiment - this is exactly similar in principle to the levitation of the human body, which has been so often described by eye-witnesses, and which you may have seen yourselves. The Earl of Dunraven told me that he had seen Mr. Home carried out of a third-story window and in at another, and he has repeated the same statement over his own signature; as have other noblemen and gentlemen of repute. The Catholic records contain many instances of the same phenomenon; and in Mr. Upham's *History of Salem Witchcraft* you will find a case where the body of Margaret Rule was so raised, in the presence of several witnesses. *The London Spiritualist* of November 19th, 1875, has a very interesting article entitled " Irdhi-Pada "—a name given to levitation by the Hindus, and meaning the Divine Foot. It has been known for centuries in that wonderful country of India, where what we call *Modern Spiritualism* was familiar to the Brahmins, ages before the Christian era. In the 4th century, Fah-Hian, a Chinese pilgrim whose local and geographical accounts have been continued as perfectly accurate, and whose evidence is, therefore, competent as to other matters, says that " Rahats (or, as we would style them in English, the Adepts) continually fly "; and again, " the men of that country frequently see persons come flying to the temple (apparently Ellora); the religious men occupying the upper chambers are constantly on the wing ". (See *Beal's Travels of Fah-Hian*.)

Oriental magic also gives to its adepts the power to make themselves invisible; as I can testify from personal experience, it having twice happened to me to witness the phenomenon. They can also extricate their spiritual bodies from their encasement of flesh, and go in them wheresoever they like. This phenomenon, in view of its frequent occurrence in all parts of the world, and establishment by a mass of evidence absolutely irrefutable, will hardly be doubted. Mrs. Hardinge Britten herself has, within the past few weeks, published a full account of her experience in this direction, both in her own person and that of others whom she has known. The most curious part of this affair of the double is the actual power of the spirit-body to exert muscular force, and do the same things with its hands as the physical members could; as, for instance, the moving of ponderable objects, the shaking of hands, the wrestling or struggling with a person, and even the commission of murder with deadly weapons. I have seen a double myself, in broad daylight, moving through a crowd like any other person, and carrying a parcel in its hand, when, to my certain knowledge, the real man was not in this country.

.In the course of my studies, I have given some little attention to this matter of the 'double', myself, and one night succeeded in obtaining a remarkable practical proof. I had been intensely engaged upon the analysis of a certain philosophical hypothesis until a very late hour of the night. Finally the work was done; and, leaving the room of my fellow-student, I retired to my own apartments. Before falling asleep, it occurred to me that, by the addition of just two words at the end of the final sentence, the whole train of thought would be much more lucidly presented. I determined to see what my double could do. I fell asleep with this purpose in my mind. The next morning, upon examining the MS., I found, to my gratification, that these two words had been added - one plainly written in my own handwriting, and the other begun but running into a scrawl, as if the power had gradually dissipated. Apparently, my double had passed out of one locked room into another locked room, in a different part of the building, and done what I had willed it to do before I lost my consciousness. In corroboration of this hypothesis, my fellow-student, before I had had time to mention the fact, told me of my appearance in the room, and my busying myself, in the dark, at the table where the manuscript lay. To say nothing of illustrations of the power of causing written communications to appear without a visible amanuensis, which is common to magicians and mediums, and which, as we have seen, can be done by the human double, as well as by the disembodied human spirit; or of portraits or other paintings, to which the same remark applies,- I will mention a most curious exhibition of will-power, the like of which I have neither read nor heard among the medium class - I refer to the engraving of letters upon metal or mineral substances, without tools or batteries of any kind. Francescari, the musician, who traveled extensively throughout India, relates the following incident: One day, being in a jeweller's shop in Lahore, he saw a gentleman importuning the proprietor to finish a piece of work on a snuffbox, which he particularly wished finished that day, as it was intended for a birthday gift. The man declared it to be impossible, as he had a number of jobs of engraving to do for other customers, each of whom was in as great a hurry as the gentleman himself. The latter pressed him still more, but in vain. At last a person sitting in a corner of the room quietly approached, and addressing the jeweller in Hindustani, told him to take the order, as the other things should be finished within a quarter of an hour. The jeweller stared, and asked him if he was a magician, to say such things. The stranger simply told him to bring his tray of jewelry; and, holding each bracelet, ring, box, or brooch in his hand, in turn, to *think of* what thing he had been ordered to do to it. He complied, and Francescari declares that instantly each was done as neatly as the best engraver or goldsmith could have done it.

Again: In a certain European city lived a famous general, who had won renown for himself by his military skill. He devotedly loved his family, but received only base ingratitude in return; for, upon his dying suddenly, they "shoved him underground " without having the decency to erect even a small stone to mark his grave. His companions in arms were so indignant that they took up a subscription, purchased a marble slab, and had it set up; but as some differences arose as to the inscription, it remained for a few days un engraved. One afternoon, however, two persons, of whom one was an adept in magic, strolling through the cemetery, noticed the blank stone; and, the story being told to the adept, that person laid a hand upon the marble, gazed at it for a few moments without telling the other what was to be done, and as the companion turned away and walked off to examine a neighbouring grave, the stone was suddenly covered with a lengthy inscription setting forth the name, age, time of decease, titles and services of the deceased. The letters were cut deep, and were gilded. I have the names of all the parties to this affair, but am under obligation to suppress them for the present, as the family are still living. I have seen only one exhibition of this kind. It occurred last summer in Boston. I was holding in my hand a moss-rose and admiring its beauty and fragrance, when before my eyes there jumped out from its heart a heavy, plain gold ring, which cleared my hand and fell upon the floor. This ring was subsequently given to an editor to examine and satisfy himself that it was without a mark, inside or outside. I examined it also, and found it as I describe. The editor was then told to look at it again; and, finding it still as plain as before, he closed his hand upon it, hold it for a half-minute, and then being requested to inspect it for the third time, he discovered inside, this inscription - *To our Brother* - followed by a triangle, a well-known kabalistic symbol. The letters were cut as clean and sharp as any graver's tool could have made them, and they remain to this day. The editor wears the ring upon his finger, and at the proper time will give his report of the phenomenon.

Let us turn now to another form of manifestation familiar among Oriental magicians, and just becoming known in this country, viz.: the apparent passage of a human body through solid walls or doors. In the VIIIth Chapter of Acts, you will find a long account of Simon the Magician, or, as he is commonly called, Simon Magus. According to the *Bible*, he possessed wonderful powers, for, as it is stated, the people of Samaria " all gave heed, from the least to the greatest, saying this man is the great power of God. And to him they had regard, because that of long time he had bewitched them with sorceries ". De Foe, the author of the immortal *Robinson Crusoe*, says in his work entitled, *A System of Magic*, which appeared in London in 1728, "the meaning is evident, this man has done such great and strange things, showed such miracles, such wonders, that none but the great power of God could enable him to do; and therefore it is certain that he is aided and assisted by the great power of God ". He further refers to the power ascribed to Simon to "fly up in the air". Now it happens that we have the testimony of two of three Fathers of the Christian Church as to the powers enjoyed by this remarkable magician, among which was this very faculty of passing through solid substances. Clemens Romanus, in his *Recognitionex*, (Lib. II, Cap. 9), and Anastasius Sinaita, in his *Quaestio* 20, tell us that: " When and to whom he pleased he made himself invisible; he created a man out of air; he passed through rocks and mountains without encountering an obstacle; he threw himself from a precipice uninjured; he flew along in the air; he flung himself in the fire without being burned. Bolts and chains were impotent to detain him. He animated statues, so that they appeared to every beholder to be men and women; he made all the furniture of the house and the table to change places as required, without a visible mover; he metamorphosed his countenance and visage into that of another person; he could make himself into a sheep, or a goat, or a serpent; he walked through the streets attended with a multitude of strange figures, which he affirmed to be the souls of the departed; he made trees and branches of trees suddenly to spring up where he pleased; he set up and deposed kings at will; he caused a sickle to go into a field of corn, which unassisted would mow twice as fast as the most industrious reaper."

The *Bible* says that he offered the apostles money to teach him their gift of working miracles, but one would be at a loss to understand why one so magnificently gifted should have made such a proposition, unless he chose to believe Clemens, who, in his *Constitutiones Apostolici*, explained it by saying that" in his sorceries he was obliged to employ tedious ceremonies and incantations; whereas the apostles appeared to effect their wonders by barely speaking a word". This is a neat Patristic puff of the Apostolic magicians, is *it not?*

Let the student of Spiritualism note the multifarious forms of what we have been accustomed to call mediumship, exhibited in this one magician's endowments, and the further fact that neither in the *Bible*, nor by the Fathers is he described as a medium. On the contrary, the evidence goes to show that he could do all these things as he chose and when he chose. In fact, I have somewhere seen an extract from his own writings - a letter addressed to an Emperor, whose name has escaped me, in which he claims to exercise these powers at will. How he made his body become so that he could pass through solid rocks and lesser barriers, is for us to discover if we can. We have the opportunity for comparison in the cases of Mrs. Compton of Havana, the Potts boys of Harrisburg, and other mediums of our day. A short time ago, I received a letter from a gentleman in Massachusetts to the effect that his brother, a young man of twenty, had, greatly to his own dissatisfaction as well as that of the whole family, been developed as a most remarkable medium. Every phase of mediumship described in my various published writings had been exemplified in his person, and, among others, this of penetrating through solid substances. The family had bound him securely with tarred ropes and with spool-cotton, sealing every knot with wax; placed him in a chair inside a home-made cabinet of deal boards; screwed the cabinet-door fast; then tied the whole box about with 80 feet of tarred rope, the knots of which were sealed also; and, the room being darkened, in 27 minutes they found the medium and chair, outside the cabinet, without a single seal having been broken either on the boy or the cabinet. Each time this experiment was tried, they discovered him in a profound catalepsy, as I found Mrs. Compton, and, to all appearance, dead but life gradually returned to his frame, and he finally became as animated as ever.

Mrs. Hyzer, the public speaker, tells me that one of the Potts brothers was thus passed through a sealed cabinet, and, after long search, was found buried beneath the mattresses of a bed, in an upper room, in the same profound trance as the others I have described. One curious feature of the case is that neither mattresses nor bed-clothes were in the slightest degree disturbed.

Mrs. Thayer, the flower medium of Boston, has had the same thing happen to her, and you have all read of the alleged transportation of Mrs. Guppy from her own house to the dark séance of the Williams mediums, where, upon hearing a noise and turning up the gas, the company discovered her standing upon the table around which they sat, with her shoes off, her dress partly unfastened, and pen and memorandum-book in her hands - as, according to her declaration, she had stood in her own apartment, two miles away, a moment before. Of course, I cannot vouch for this case at all, not having been an eye- witness; nor would I quote it or any of the others coming within this category, but for the curious corroboration they offer to the story of Simon Magus, and other biblical and profane records of magical power. If I had time I might point you to numerous instances, scattered throughout the *Bible,* of this same power of being taken to pieces, so to speak, and transported from place to place; but I am compelled to put aside a multitude of facts occurring in ancient and modern epochs, and so must refer you to the work of Dr. Eugene Crowell, which shows the identity between Ancient Christianity and Modern Spiritualism.

It is not the purpose of this lecture to string together a lot of marvelous tales to amuse the fancy or please the ear, but simply to point out the fact that our studies of these modern phenomena have been in the wrong direction. Like our scientists and theologians, we have looked to the right and left, above and below, for explanations of natural law, but forgotten the Past. We have not seemed to imagine that what Hume calls our " ignorant ancestors," could have known anything worth our while to examine. We have been as silly as the traveler who should attempt to study the language of an unfamiliar country, or its geography, without asking if there were such a thing as a grammar or a dictionary, a vocabulary or a map, in existence. We have been attending circles, week after week, month after month, and year after year, gaping at fresh wonders, swallowing what was put into our mouths, and never turning over old books, nor ransacking old libraries, to see what our progenitors knew about this sort of thing. We have been ever ready to answer the sneers and taunts of our orthodox friends by quoting to them the scores of passages in Scripture which show, not only the appearance of every one of our familiar manifestations, from the raps to "materialization," among the Hebrews, but the important enunciation that these same signs should follow the true "Christian" ever after. Here are two large volumes written by my learned friend Dr. Crowell, to carry out this very idea. But neither he, nor a soul among us dreamed, until very recently, that what we had heard called Oriental Magic was the self-same thing as American Spiritualism, only better in every respect. Not one of us dreamed that these occult forces of which the scientists, and we ourselves, echoing them, have prated about, could be controlled by the human will-power to produce every manifestation known to us, and scores that we have not yet witnessed.

Observe, please, that I use the collective pronoun, we, for I take as much blame, and more, to myself than I give to others for this stupid neglect. I became a believer in Spiritualistic phenomena in 1852, and took an active part in aiding the movement, by writing, speaking, and organizing a society to establish the Dodworth Hall meetings. From that time to this, I have never known the moment when my faith weakened one particle, and when my present critics assail me as a renegade, they - well, they talk like most people who write about things of which they are ignorant. No, so far as belief in the reality of spirit intercourse is concerned, I yield to none of you in earnestness. But, as for being satisfied to remain one instant longer, as I had for twenty-odd years, a Spiritualist, by which I mean an unquestioning believer that every genuine *spirit* manifestation is produced by disembodied human spirits, when I had learnt to the contrary, I would not think of it. I would as soon have remained in the Presbyterian Church, in which I was baptized and reared, after reading the *Anacalypsis* of Godfrey Higgins, or Ennemoser's *History of Magic*.

Since I had the misfortune to be thrust into a somewhat conspicuous position in connection with spiritualistic investigations, I have had to pay the penalty in a very large correspondence with persons in many countries. They, one and all, ask me to give them a list of books to road which will acquaint them with this subject of Magic and the Elementary Spirits. To such, I particularly recommend Ennemoser's *History of Magic*, in 2 volumes, translated from the German by William Howitt. Mr. Howitt's own *History of the Supernatural* embodies pretty nearly the same facts. Sir Charles Napier's *Indian Recollections* comprise some particulars about Hindu Magicians; as Lane's *Modern Egyptians* does much about the magicians of the land of the Pharaohs (some of which stories I have quoted in my *People from the Other World*). Osburne's *Camp and Court of Runjeet Singh*, a very rare book, if my own experience be considered, tells us how the Hindu Fakirs allow themselves to be buried alive for weeks together, and after the end of, say, 30 to 40 days, resume their vitality upon being exhumed and rubbed, with certain attendant magical ceremonies. Speaking of this, some of you may have recently seen, in the N. Y. World, a letter addressed to me by an ex Lieutenant-Colonel of the General Staff in India, a brother of the Earl of Ellenboro, testifying to having himself served as one of a Committee selected by the Rajah of Puttiala to superintend a ceremony of this kind, and to the fact that, at the expiration of 30 days, the fakir was dug up and revived.

I have received, through the kindness of a gentleman in Tennessee, a catalogue of nearly 2,000 works in German, which treat of this subject of Magic in all its branches - among which are included Mesmerism and Spiritualism. The French language contains many valuable works also in some of which I have found evidence of the nature and powers of the Elementary Spirits sufficient to satisfy the most skeptical. By some strange mental blindness, the Catholic clergy have assisted in the production of a series of works each of which is a stick to break their own sectarian heads. I refer to the several volumes of the Chevalier des Mousseaux. The theory of the Vatican was that it was only necessary to show what wonders magic could produce, and then call them all devilish, to have the public run away from the magicians into the arms of Mother Church. To the end that nothing might be lacking to make the record complete, the most secret treasures of the Vatican were spread before the devoted author, and the consequence is, such a collection of facts for us heretics as we can find nowhere else in literature. They show us the clue to every single miracle of the *Bible*, and every phenomenon of Modern Spiritualism, and instead of attracting us to Rome, they make us wish to run away from her to Karnac and Thebes as fast as we can. Read des Mousseaux by the light of Ennemoser, and be wise.

If you would know about the magic of the Greeks and Romans, and their mythological systems, where can you go amiss in the classical authors whose works are all to be had in English translations? Prescott tells you a little about ancient Peruvian magic, and Brosseur de Bourbourg much about that of the Quiches.

So you see, friends, that knowledge of Spiritualism, like knowledge of things of far less human concern, can be had as the price of hard work. We can't learn how raps are caused, furniture moved, communications written, pictures painted, voices made: how clairvoyants see, flowers and birds are brought into closed rooms, and mediums are carried out of them; or how the spirits of the ,the dead, and of those not dead, are materialized; nor how the elementaries approach, influence, control, pervert, and seduce mediums, by reading *Spiritual Scientists*, *Banners of Light*, or *Religio-Philosophical Journals*, which, however valuable as journals, are of necessity mainly current news: we must study books, and many of them, and the right ones.

If I have been so fortunate as to have commanded your thoughtful attention, you will have perceived the important - the *vital* distinction there is between the relation of the magician and that of the medium, towards the spirit-world. The magician - the *wise*, the *Educated* man - not only knows the subtle potencies of Nature, but also how to employ them to effect his purpose. He not only is familiar with the various races which inhabit the Inner World, - or what the two English Professors, Tait and Balfour Stewart, call the "*Unseen Universe*" - and with the location, employments and destiny of our ancestors, but by his superb power can make the former do his bidding, as we govern a child or break a horse. He summons the latter to approach and tell him whatever he wishes to know. The true magician has not only knowledge of his powers, but faith to use them - that faith which the Apostle Peter, sinking in the waters, lacked; and that faith which Jesus, one of the greatest of Kabalists, said would enable its possessor to cause a mountain to be removed to another place. To him there is no accident, no miracle in Nature, but every thing happens in obedience to law; and, while suffering Nature to perform his wonders for him, he stands beside her and prompts her as to what she shall do.

On the other hand, the medium, instead of being an active ruler of the elements, is their passive victim. Surrounded by the invisible but all potent currents of the Astral Light, saturated by them throughout his sensitive being, he is borne hither and thither, wheresoever their blind impulse leads, or they are directed by the irresponsible beings who people their depths. He is as incapable of stemming these currents, as is the chip the river upon whose surface it floats; or the dried leaf the wind upon which it is borne and tossed about. Before he knows his danger, it has overtaken and subdued him; and nothing but an innate purity, capable of withstanding every contamination, can save him from the chance of moral perversion and physical exhaustion. If there is a single weak joint in his moral harness, the Elementaries will find it and reach the vital parts of his character; and this is what constitutes the danger of mediumship for physical manifestations. Run over in your minds the names of all the people of this class of whose private life you know something definite, and recall how many of them are entirely truthful, pure, temperate, and self-helpful. There are a few - far be it from me to say otherwise. But the greater portion are the reverse. Pity and excuse them as we may, out of love for the Cause, the fact remains that, in too many cases, they *are* objects of pity and require excuse. Does this mean nothing? Is there no cause for such a state of things? Let Spiritualists reflect. It is time. If we mean to hold our own against the Materialists (in and out of the churches), we must fortify our philosophy so that it shall have no weak side. We must make it so that it may he turned about, and inside out, and show no speck or flaw. We cannot expect others to make the same excuses and allowances for the misbehaviour of mediums and their patrons; their fanciful theories, and their unsavory social systems; or the contradictions, inconsistencies and absurdities of their communications. We must know *why* all these things are, and discover the remedy. The key and the panacea, I am persuaded, are in Eastern Magic, and, as opportunity offers, I mean to study it. I am urged to this, not merely from a selfish desire to pry into the secrets of Nature, but, also, by the infinite compassion which I feel for the hundreds and thousands of mediums subjected to every misfortune as a consequence of their mediumship. I feel a sincere desire to give what little help I can to the good, the earnest, the blameless people who lean upon Spiritualism as their mainstay and prop; and who trust it to give them that sweetest of all consolations, the assurance of an immortal life beyond the grave, where meeting and parting are known no more.

> "Never here, forever there,
> Where all parting, pain, and care,
> And death, and time shall disappear —
> Forever there, but never here!
> The horologe of Eternity
> Sayeth this incessantly — Forever—never !
> Never—forever "

www.ingramcontent.com/pod-product-compliance
Lightning Source LLC
LaVergne TN
LVHW041503070426
835507LV00009B/777